Doctor Owlkin and The H.O.M.E. Team
(Help Or Motivate Everybody!)

Celebrating Our Differences and Diversity with Inclusion

Our Mission: The Doctor Owlkin book series was created **_to raise the self-esteem and confidence of children with special needs, disabilities, or differences and teach other children acceptance and inclusion of those with differences or disabilities_**. Even though others may be "different," we find that inside everybody just wants to be loved, encouraged, accepted, appreciated, and included!

Doctor Owlkin, the members of The H.O.M.E. Team, and the animal characters in the books become the heroes who find a way to make their diversity or differences an attribute or advantage. The H.O.M.E. Team is led by wise old **Doctor Owlkin** and loving **Nurse Sharky**, who bring together their helpers. The first four books in the series tell the amazing stories of each of the helpers. The H.O.M.E. Team includes **Trouble**, a Bloodhound who was born with extraordinarily long and useful ears; **King Tux**, a tiny cat who has a BIG personality and smarts; **Pirate**, a lop-eared rabbit with only one eye who sees the world in a unique way; and **Goldie**, a Golden Retriever who was born with 3 ½ legs but doesn't let that stop her from being a hero. Each of these characters has adapted and developed special skills – their "superpowers" – that allow them to uplift and encourage others to be the best they can be, regardless of their differences!

In subsequent books, The H.O.M.E. Team goes out into the community to help other animals. Each book addresses a new "difference" to teach children why that character is special, and that we are all "different and unique" in some way.

As **Doctor Owlkin** always reminds the team, **"It's WHOOOOOO you are on the inside that matters most!"**

Dedicated in loving memory of
Laxmi Devi Agusala and Ike Perlman

Edited by Gary M. Hardee, PhD
Consultant: Annalise Sansouci, CCLS

Website – www.HelpOrMotivateEverybody.org

Facebook – https://www.facebook.com/DrOwlkin

YouTube – https://www.youtube.com/watch?v=mTV7h_BXjEU

Instagram – https://www.instagram.com/dr.owlkin/?hl=en

Twitter – https://twitter.com/TheHOMETeamHel1

Linkedin – https://www.linkedin.com/company/help-or-motivate-everybody

ISBN: 978-1-7368708-0-8
1st Edition

Every picture has a hidden heart. Can you find it?

Kindly old Doctor Owlkin smiles. He is happy.

He watches his dear friend, Nurse Sharky, put red poppy wildflowers in an old blue vase that someone threw away.

The red poppies make H.O.M.E. *feel* like home.

H.O.M.E. is what Doctor Owlkin and Nurse Sharky named their new clinic. There is a big sign over the front door. It says H.O.M.E. on top and below reads Help Or Motivate Everybody. H.O.M.E. is a long, cream-cake-colored building with blue-frosting shutters. Big windows welcome in the sun.

It was an abandoned old motel outside of Hopeville.

H.O.M.E. was a forgotten place hidden in Willow and Oak trees.

A secret place where beetles and ladybugs crawl through Indian grass. Where earthworms wriggle in red dirt. Field mice nest in straw. Cottontail rabbits hop over clay mounds. Blue clipper butterflies float over wisteria flowers.

Doctor Owlkin and Nurse Sharky turned this forgotten place into a happy place.

A safe place.

A H.O.M.E. for forgotten animals.

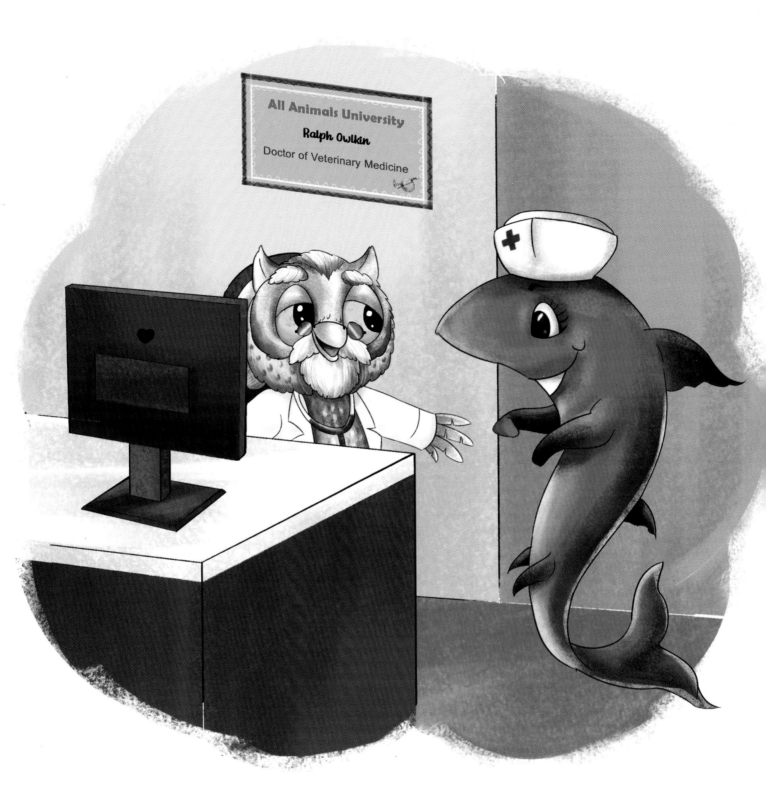

"I'm so excited to have a place where we can help animals in need. I know we can help lots of them!" says Doctor Owlkin.

"I'm so thrilled that we are finally open," Nurse Sharky exclaims. "Now we just need to find the right helpers."

"Whoooo yes," Doctor Owlkin hoots as only owls can do—a loud beep interrupts Doctor Owlkin.

It comes from his new computer. The computer was a welcome gift from the animals of Hopeville.

"Whoooo!" Doctor Owlkin hoots again. "An alert!"

Someone needs help!

He reads a message from Mr. McGruffy, the grumpy grocer in Hopeville.

"It looks like Mr. McGruffy needs us at his store," says Doctor Owlkin.

"Our first alert. Let's go!" Nurse Sharky shouts.

In Hopeville, Doctor Owlkin and Nurse Sharky pull up in their special H.O.M.E. mobile.

A scraggly, skinny Bloodhound sits near Mr. McGruffy. Other shop owners surround the scrawny, shaking pup.

"Whooooo, look at that pup's long, long ears!" says Doctor Owlkin.

The ears are as long as the pup's body. They are so long they spread onto the ground even when the pup stands up!

"That poor hound sure looks embarrassed and scared!" says Nurse Sharky.

"This bony mutt has been digging through the trash. She knocks over all the dumpsters!" grouchy Mr. McGruffy grumbles. "She has no tags or collar, doesn't know where she lives."

Mr. McGruffy hopes Doctor Owlkin can help.

Mr. McGruffy adds, "I heard you just opened that H.O.M.E. clinic. I thought you could take her and get this mutt out of our hair!"

Doctor Owlkin nods. Nurse Sharky slowly walks toward the scared pup.

The dog's long ears begin to rise. She starts a low growl.

"Grrrrrrrrr."

Nurse Sharky whispers, "Now, now little doggy, everything will be just fine."

But the Bloodhound backs up slowly and growls again.

"Grrrrrrr."

And then in a flash, those extraordinarily long ears whirl upward. They flap like the wings of a seagull!

She takes off and soars past Mr. McGruffy's legs and into the alley.

The shop owners have seen her do this many times. They begin to shout and chase her.

Nurse Sharky stops them.

"Everybody, stay here," she says with authority.

She walks quietly, carefully into the alley.

She can't see the pup but hears a low growl.

"Grrrrrrrrr."

Nurse Sharky knows what it is like to be scared. She knows she can't catch this pup. When the pup's ears start flapping, she flies like a bird!

What should I do? Nurse Sharky wonders.

Ah ha, she thinks. *I must get her to trust me.*

Slowly and carefully Nurse Sharky walks closer to where the Bloodhound has backed herself into a corner.

"Easy now. Nice doggy. What's your name?" Nurse Sharky asks softly.

"Grrrrrrrrr," the pup growls.

Nurse Sharky pulls a doggy snack from her pocket. She places it on the ground.

The hungry pup gobbles up the dog snack.

"I am only here to help," Nurse Sharky says kindly. "I know how it feels to be hungry and alone. Little darling, how did you become so lost?"

She sees the pup's ears rise. She is ready to soar off again. Nurse Sharky hears another "grrrrrrrr."

She puts another doggy snack on the ground and steps back.

Nurse Sharky says, "I can tell you're really smart. That's why those shop owners can't catch you! I bet you could help us when we find other lost animals."

Her soothing voice calms the pup. The pup's ears droop. She gobbles more doggy snacks.

Finally, the pup decides to speak.

"I don't know my name. All I remember is being taken to a new home in the back of a truck," she says.

"The crate I was in fell off the back of the truck and I fell out and hit my head really hard. It was so loud. Cars were swerving, tires screeching and horns honking," she tells Nurse Sharky.

The pup continues, "I was scared. I ran down the hill into the forest. It was so thick my ears kept getting caught in the branches."

"When it got dark I hid in a hole in a really tall tree," the pup says. "There were so many noises all around me. Wolves howling. Little animals scurrying by me all night. I was really scared and I didn't sleep a wink."

"Oh my, you poor pup," Nurse Sharky says. She sees the big bump on the pup's head.

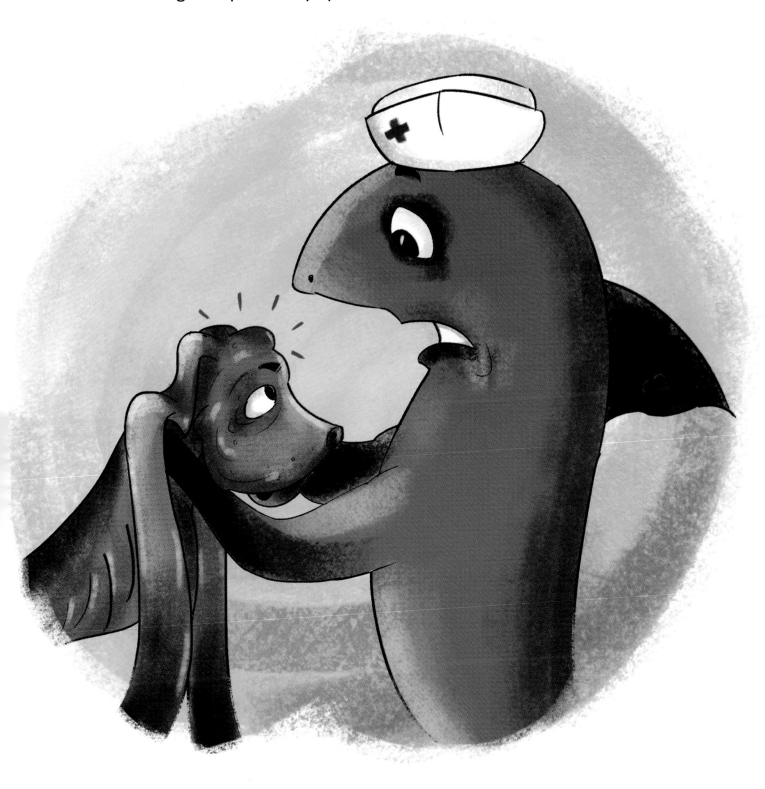

The pup doesn't even notice that Nurse Sharky has moved closer.

"I finally found food in Mr. McGruffy's dumpster. But that just made all of the shop owners angry," says the pup.

"They chased me but my long ears could hear them coming and I was able to fly away!"

The pup hangs her head low and begins to cry. "Now I don't know anyone. I have no place to live," she whimpers. "I didn't mean to make a mess. I can't remember anything. I don't know what to do."

Nurse Sharky is close enough to stroke the pup's long soft ears. "Why don't you let Doctor Owlkin look at this bump on your head?" Nurse Sharky asks.

Together, they walk out of the alley. They see Doctor Owlkin and Mr. McGruffy.

"There she is!" one shop owner shouts. "She's a *bad dog*.
She's *trouble*!"

The pup's ears rise. She looks ready to soar away again.
Nurse Sharky's squeaky laugh makes her stop.

"Hey," she says. "*Trouble*! I love it. Let's name her
Trouble! Come on, Trouble."

She lets out another squeaky laugh. It makes everybody smile, even Trouble!

Doctor Owlkin kneels down to rub his hand across Trouble's head. He feels the big bump.

"Whoooo, my, you might have a concussion," Doctor Owlkin hoots. "Where is your home?"

"I don't know. I can't remember," Trouble replies.

"Whooooo, you might have what is called amnesia," the wise old doctor says. "That can happen when you have a really hard hit to the head." Doctor Owlkin tells Trouble that amnesia is when you have a hard time remembering things. "Most of the time, it doesn't last long, but it can be very scary," he says.

Doctor Owlkin also knows how scary it is to be alone.

"Why don't you come to our H.O.M.E. You can stay with us as long as it takes for your memory to come back. Or, better yet, we can help find your family!" Doctor Owlkin exclaims.

Doctor Owlkin turns to grumpy Mr. McGruffy and says, "Thank you for calling us. We'll take care of Trouble."

Mr. McGruffy looks at his feet and mutters, "Well I shouldn't have gotten so mad at her. I didn't know she needed help. She could've just asked."

Trouble says softly to Mr. McGruffy, "I'm sorry. I didn't know who to trust."

Doctor Owlkin, Nurse Sharky, and Trouble climb into the H.O.M.E. mobile.

Doctor Owlkin says, "Trouble, when we return to the clinic, I'll send emails out to all the shelters. Hopefully, we can find out where your home is."

Trouble's long ears perk up. Each one twirls tightly into a point. They look like two long fingers.

"I can help with that. Believe it or not, I type really fast with my ears," she says.

Nurse Sharky gives Trouble a puzzled look. She laughs.

"I don't know how I know it, but I do!" Trouble says.

Nurse Sharky exclaims, "I'm sure there are many ways your ears can come in handy! What may seem different or unusual about someone can be one of the best things about them!"

Doctor Owlkin smiles. He is happy. He knows Trouble is going to love her new H.O.M.E.

THE END

Book Two

Learn the story of the next member of

The H.O.M.E. Team

"King Tux"